Life Lessons in Business:
Wisdom from Warren E. Buffett & L.A."Davy" Davidson

by Gwyn Davidson Larsen

Life Lessons in Business: Wisdom from
Warren E. Buffett & L.A."Davy" Davidson

ISBN 978-0-9798723-0-3

Second printing, 2007

Proceeds from this book are donated to
The Davy Foundation
www.thedavyfoundation.org

Life Lessons in Business:

Wisdom from Warren E. Buffett & L.A."Davy" Davidson

by Gwyn Davidson Larsen

To my precious grandparents who told me I would write someday – and they were right – I dedicate this book to you. Your profound influence will be felt forever. I love you and miss you.

Enjoy! This book is only the beginning.

Acknowledgements

One thing that every single person said to me about my Granddad was "how very much he loved his wife." That legacy of his love for his family will remain with me forever. Without question, I owe an enormous amount of gratitude, first to Granddad and Grandmother for giving me their journals and every newspaper article ever written, (so it seemed), and for making me promise this book would come to fruition.

There are no words to adequately express my deep appreciation and respect for Mr. Warren E. Buffett, Mr. Jack Byrne, and Mr. Tony Nicely. Next to Mr. Harvey Graham,

Gwyn Davidson Larsen at her desk in July 2007.

Life Lessons in Business:
Wisdom from Warren E. Buffett & L.A."Davy" Davidson

by Gwyn Davidson Larsen

To my precious grandparents who told me I would write someday – and they were right – I dedicate this book to you. Your profound influence will be felt forever. I love you and miss you.

Enjoy! This book is only the beginning.

Foreword by Warren E. Buffett

I can think of 100 wonderful adjectives to describe Lorimer Davidson. But if I used every one of them I would not be doing him justice.

Obviously, he was a wonderful businessman and, as you know, a wonderful grandfather. To me, however, he was a friend and teacher, almost without peer. How many other business people would have taken precious time on a Saturday to spend four hours with a 20-year-old who had wandered in off the street? And especially a 20-year-old who in no conceivable way could be expected to reciprocate the kindness and wisdom that was to be imparted to him.

From that day in early 1951, my life developed far differently than if I hadn't met Davy. What I learned in those four hours was more valuable than the knowledge that I had acquired in all of my college years. Indeed, Berkshire and I would not even be in the insurance business now if it hadn't been for Davy's initial instruction and encouragement. Within months after our meeting, I launched my career in Omaha as a securities salesman by telling people about GEICO. My reputation was established by this recommendation. Imagine the difference in my life if I had initially been encouraging investment in the stock of some public utility or mutual fund.

For the rest of his life, Davy continued to be my teacher and friend. Finally in 1995 I talked to him about my hope to buy the rest of GEICO for Berkshire Hathaway. If I went ahead he would incur a large capital gains tax which otherwise would be avoided by his estate. Almost anyone else would have advised delay. But Davy's reaction was immediate: "It will be good for GEICO and for Berkshire Hathaway – I'm all for it."

Gwyn, your grandfather was a very rare man and one all of us should emulate.

Warren E. Buffett

July 25, 2007

Captain Lorimer A. Davidson, Canadian Army, during World War II.

L.A. "Davy" Davidson

My grandfather, Lorimer A. "Davy" Davidson was born in Canada, the son of an investment banker.

Granddad went to Wall Street to embark on his dream career as a trader and a bond salesman. He was highly successful. He had a seat on the floor of the New York Stock Exchange.

He met and fell in love with my beautiful grandmother, Betty, a talented Broadway dancer. They remained in Manhattan until 1940, when my grandfather returned to Canada to join the Canadian Army as an officer during the war. Following his honorable discharge in 1946, my grandparents and their son, my father, made their home in Washington D.C. At the age of 48, Granddad became an American citizen.

On my granddad's first day on the job with E.R. Jones and Company he made his first call to GEICO® (Government Employees Insurance Company). The rest, as they say, is history – a wonderful history of an honorable gentleman who loved his wife, his family, his country, his beloved GEICO, and his friends.

Acknowledgements

O ne thing that every single person said to me about my Granddad was "how very much he loved his wife." That legacy of his love for his family will remain with me forever. Without question, I owe an enormous amount of gratitude, first to Granddad and Grandmother for giving me their journals and every newspaper article ever written, (so it seemed), and for making me promise this book would come to fruition.

There are no words to adequately express my deep appreciation and respect for Mr. Warren E. Buffett, Mr. Jack Byrne, and Mr. Tony Nicely. Next to Mr. Harvey Graham,

Gwyn Davidson Larsen at her desk in July 2007.

who has passed on, they were my Granddad's best friends. He loved them like his very own children and he followed their success with much joy and pride. Occasionally, when one of your children gets a bit off center you have to help them out – and my granddad could give you a lecture, one you never wanted to hear again. (I know this first hand.) All three of these honorable men have been true and loyal to their word, and their kindness is unsurpassed.

Also, many thanks to everyone, and I mean everyone, who helped at GEICO with this project. You are all wonderful and I thank you.

It is vitally important to me to thank my son, Greg, who helped, encouraged, edited, and, in many ways, did a lot of work to make this happen. Greg Larsen is a genius. I pray you'll meet him someday and your life will be better for it.

For my daughter, Lori, my gratitude is immense. Lori reminds me so much of her late father. Lori worked, organized, filed, researched and found pictures. Lori Aston is also a genius and she's an angel on this earth. Lori loved, as did Greg, my grandparents and that love was returned ten-fold. I hope you also have a chance to meet Lori Aston. She is amazing!

To love two men – at the same time, – is my reality. After 24 years of marriage and four children, you just plan your life growing old together. That was not mine to have. When my husband died of CJD, I never dreamed I would love again. My husband now, who lost his wife after 28 years of marriage and three children, felt the same.

Somebody was looking out for both of us. John not only gave me my life back, if you will, but he also inspired me to keep the promise. Without John, not one page of this book would be completed. Without question he has been my greatest cheerleader. I love you. Thank you.

Thanks to my parents, Tom and Nancy, and my children, Jonalynn, Greg, Heather, Lori, Keriann, Emily, Ashley and their spouses and my grandchildren, for believing in me. I love you all, heart to heart. Last, but not least, a huge thanks to Michael Goodwin and Dr. Sharman Sutherland.

"The heart speaks the language only the soul understands." May your soul be touched in some way as you learn from the wisdom of these two remarkable men.

Always,
Gwyn

Table of Contents

Origins..3

Tribute from Warren E. Buffett 7

Getting Started.....................................9

Take a Taxi Home, or Not?....................11

Don't Get Swept Up in Excitement 15

True Customer Service 17

A Promise Kept...................................21

Finding out Everything.........................25

Coca-Cola Six Pack..............................31

Being a Pro 33

Competition – Change is Necessary..............37

Cost Control 39

Great Expectations..............................41

Teamwork & $20 Gold 41

Freedom, Right, and Choice 45

Giving Back......................................49

K.I.S.S..51

Survival by Adaptation and
   Thinking Outside the Box 53

Management: Which Way? 57

Stop, Smile, and say Hello 61

Chip 65

The Passing of a Great Man 67

Favorite Quotes of Grandad......................71

About the Author.................................82

"It is not the title that maketh the person, but the person that maketh the title honorable."
                                        – *Cicero*

"Think to Thank."

                                        – *Anonymous*

Baby Gwyn and her grandfather Davy in the fall of 1958.

Origins

This journey began in the fall of 1958. I was born on my grandparents' wedding anniversary. My grandfather called me his "lucky charm." As I grew up, I had a very unique and cherished experience. I was taught at his knee about the business and investment world. I met many nice people who were, and are, "big shots!"

It wasn't until the mid 70's, when Mr. Lorimer Arthur "Davy" Davidson – my Granddad – began sharing with me, not only his amazing knowledge and wisdom, but also true stories of "life lessons" in business. I became his student and he became my teacher, asking only one promise from me: that I would contact five people before I turned fifty and then write a book.

The list included his dear friend, Warren Buffett, along with Jack Byrne, and Tony Nicely.

Warren owns GEICO. Jack was the CEO that saved GEICO, the company my grandfather had put his whole heart and soul into building, and Tony is the CEO of GEICO today. Granddad was also CEO of GEICO.

There were also two other people on that list: Phyllis, who taught me how to type, among many other things, when I would spend time at GEICO with my Granddad, and Pixie, a woman who became an amazing investor and dear friend to my Granddad.

All the calls were made, visits and toasts were given, questions were answered, and much encouragement was given to follow my heart.

Warren and Jack were especially tender. Granddad had taken them under his wing and he was so sure of their success and brilliance.

It is my Granddad, Davy Davidson, who spent nearly five hours on a Saturday, when he had gone into the office to get some extra work done, talking with then a 20-year-old young man about the insurance business. That man was Warren Buffett. The friendship and mentoring between them never stopped after that very first meeting.

They remained great friends throughout my Granddad's life. He told me that a Warren Buffett only comes along maybe once in a century and that Warren had never forgotten to thank those who had taken the time to help him.

That life lesson right there is a good reminder to all of us – thanking someone never goes out of style. This book is just the beginning of a lifetime of knowledge and wisdom, imparted over the years to hundreds of thousands of people. This book is just to get us all started, to help us remember that day in and day out we build the lives and relationships we wish to have.

I am grateful to my grandfather and to Warren, who so generously encouraged me to put these time tested truths down on paper. The first page of this book really says it all about my Granddad's credibility.

Davy Davidson was one of the greatest mentors to Warren Buffett, Jack Byrne, Tony Nicely, and, without question, to his one and only granddaughter.

What an amazing legacy he left. It is my hope that we will all be inspired by Davy's wisdom and that we are better people because of it.

The proud Davidson grandparents.

Lorimer A. "Davy" Davidson   Betty Gael Davidson

Tribute from Warren E. Buffett

BERKSHIRE HATHAWAY INC.
1440 KIEWIT PLAZA
OMAHA, NEBRASKA 68131

WARREN E. BUFFETT, CHAIRMAN

May 5, 1998
Dear Davy,

You can't imagine what a hit your message made yesterday at the annual meeting of Berkshire Hathaway shareholders. When you were talking, you could have heard a pin drop among the 8,000 people in the main room (additionally, there were a couple of overflow rooms with several thousand attendees). Needless to say, I was popping a few buttons.

I think the best way to put it is that the crowd listened to you yesterday in the same way as I listened to you 47 years ago. And thank heavens I did: What a difference the education you gave me has meant in my life.

Davy, you've been a great friend, a great teacher, and, best of all, a great model to follow. Jack, Tony and I have all accomplished far more in life because we have walked in your footsteps.

Sincerely,

Warren E. Buffett

"Do your best, not because your work is worth it, but because you are."
— Young People's Weekly

"A true friend is somebody who can make us do what we can."
— Emerson

Warren E. Buffett

Hi Dan —
Without you, my life would
have been far different. you are
a wonderful friend + teacher.
Happy Holidays!
Warren

Getting Started

The day my Granddad first told me about Mr. Warren Buffett was a bright summer morning and we were at GEICO. I had just finished the third grade, and at the beginning of the year, my grade in handwriting had been a "U." I had worked all year long to bring my penmanship grade up to an "E." Granddad was very proud of me and my effort.

It was then that Granddad brought me into the "world of excellence" and explained to me that I would know it, as I encountered it throughout my entire life.

He told me of examples of excellence in the world of business and he told me about Warren, who epitomized excellence to my grandfather.

Granddad also told me about himself and how, almost from the time he was ten or eleven years old, he had known what he wanted to do: he was going to be in the business world. He wanted to go into investment banking. He wanted to be just what his father was.

The only thing was – he wanted to do it on Wall Street, – but he was in Montreal. He didn't talk to his father about Wall Street until he was working for Hanson Brothers. He knew he had to start in Montreal first, and he did. He worked for Hanson Brothers for two years before he went to Wall Street.

"We are all manufacturers, making goods, making trouble, and making excuses."

– *Anonymous*

The President of GEICO, Leo Goodwin. When Goodwin chose to retire in 1958, he named Davy Davidson to be his successor at GEICO. *(Photo courtesy GEICO.)*

Take a Taxi Home or Not?

When Granddad started back in the securities business, after a "break for the War," he started in Washington D.C. as an institutional bond salesman for E. R. Jones. He had all the institutional business in Washington D. C. as his exclusive area. The first day he started to work, he had a list of about hundred names of companies that he was going to call on.

In the afternoon, by around 2 or 3 o'clock, it was raining. It was really miserable weather. Granddad had just gotten over pneumonia and he was tired. He had a big problem: "Do I take the taxi home, or do I call on this last name here on the list: Government Employees Insurance Company?"

He decided he would call on GEICO. Deciding to visit GEICO was the right thing to do. This wasn't a sales call, but more of an introductory call to tell them who he was and what he could do for them.

He went to the building, up to the sixth floor, gave his card to the receptionist, and told her that he would like to see whoever was handling the investment portfolio. She said she didn't know who that would be. So he asked to speak to the president of the company. She called the president, and a minute or two later, the president of GEICO came out to see my Granddad and he took him into his office.

Now remember, this was my Granddad's first day on the job. It was close to the end of the business day, and Granddad wasn't feeling one hundred percent, but he knew that deciding to visit GEICO was the right thing to do. It was an unusually amazing first interview that proved to be the first of many talks.

Neither the president, Leo Goodwin, nor the founder of GEICO, Cleaves Rhea, knew much about investment securities, but they had a great interest in learning more.

The vast majority of professionals would gladly give up a few hours of their working day to head home early, hit the golf course, run some errands, or just take some time to themselves away from work. But, my Granddad asked, "Does that really benefit them?" Granted there are always very good reasons to leave work early, but those very good reasons only come every great once in a while.

A strong work ethic is something that my Granddad often spoke of to me. In fact, he pointed out that if it wasn't for that strong work ethic, he might not have ever began a relationship with GEICO.

After World War II, Washington D.C. was a great place for businesses.

"Learn from your mistakes and then, don't repeat them."
— *Davy Davidson*

Warren E. Buffett

Dear Davy —
It's moments like this when
my memory goes back to meeting
you 42 years ago. I'll always
be grateful.
Happy Holidays!
Warn

Don't Get Swept Up in Excitement

Granddad gave some great advice in this example, one that's about himself, and I will let him tell it in his own words:

"I had developed a very bad habit of trading in the stock market. And I traded like an idiot, one who buys in the morning and sells in the afternoon. I don't remember the day that happened. I know that I had a big short position in Radio, which had gone from $200 a share to $500 a share."

"A short position—it's when you sell something you don't own and you borrow stock to deliver, and you hope to buy it back at a lower price, getting a profit. Then you return the stock to the owner. Radio was one of the darlings of Wall Street then, and everybody was trading off it, and it changed 40, 50 points a day. On the 4th of July, 1929, Betty and I went out for the weekend on a small yacht that a friend of hers in show business owned. There were six of us there, and we spent most of the weekend talking about the stock market. The next day – that would be the 5th of July – I sold out my long position, and I went short Radio. Radio promptly went up 150 points, and I got sold out at about 490, 495 something like that."

"In other words, if I'd waited until the 6th of July, I'd have made a couple hundred thousand dollars. Instead, I lost everything we had. But, I learned a lesson that was worth an awful lot: DON'T TRADE ON THE MARGIN."

"Again, my strong advice, DO NOT BUY ON MARGIN!"

– Davy Davidson

"Learn your lessons. Once."

– Davy Davidson

Anxious people crowd the entrance of the New York Stock Exchange, in October, 1929.

True Customer Service

The awful day the stock market crashed, October 15, 1929, most Americans lost a lot of their life savings, if not all of it. Granddad tells it this way:

"I was no less fortunate than the next gentlemen, but, fortunately for my customers, I had already hit rock bottom a few weeks prior. Instead of staying home and worrying about my own financial situation, I worked harder than ever to help my clientele avoid some of the same pitfalls I had found."

"The day the stock market crashed, I not only tried to help my clients, but I spent nearly 24 hours straight doing so. My interest on October 15 was in the few individual customers I had who were on margin. And, every one of them, of course, was really on the margin by the time the market closed.

So I spent that evening, and that whole night, making phone calls and visits to my clients. I even helped other salesmen make calls to their clients. Every one of them was a call for margin."

"We worked all day and all night without going home. Sleep didn't come to me until close to 5 a.m. the next morning. That was a horrific day financially for everyone. We did our best and were able to have success with some of our clients, who, at the time, had more margin to put up."

"In this day and age of 'yesterday is too late,' and 'tomorrow is not soon enough,' do we take a second out of our day to really think about our customers needs? Do we focus on the aspects of business that make us more money or on the aspects that will benefit those whose interests we represent?

Ask yourself, have I called, made a visit, or sent a card to my customers lately. Knowing and caring about your clients is a fortune far above what money will ever bring you."

Gwyn's business card.

Davy's business cards. Davy felt the cards were essential business equipment that represented you and your business, and he often wrote personal notes on the back to clients thanking them.

"This world belongs to the energetic."
— *Emerson*

"Every noble work is at first impossible."
— *Carlyle*

Warren E.
Buffett

Lorimer A. "Davy"
Davidson

A Promise Kept

From the 1950's until the death of my Granddad in 1999, most everyone involved with GEICO knew "Mr. D." It was, in fact, "his beloved GEICO." He even spent his "down time" there, even before he was the CEO. He had met this young man, by the name of Warren Buffett, on a Saturday morning when he had gone into the office to "get a few things done." He liked to be at GEICO when no one else was around, when he felt he could get more accomplished.

On a cold day in January 1951, a custodian at GEICO noticed a young man knocking on the glass at the entrance and the custodian asked my Granddad, Mr. D., if he should let the man in. Granddad said, "Give me five minutes with him and then we will nicely escort him out of the building." At the time Granddad's office was on the sixth floor.

Warren writes, and I quote: "So, on a Saturday in January, 1951, I took the train to Washington and headed to GEICO's downtown headquarters. To my dismay, the building was closed, but I pounded on the door until a custodian appeared. I asked this puzzled fellow if there was anyone in the office I could talk to, and he said he'd seen one man working on the sixth floor." *(from the 1995 Berkshire Hathaway annual report.)*

That man on the sixth floor was, of course, my Granddad, Lorimer Davidson, known to most as either

Davy Davidson, or Mr. D. – the future head of GEICO.
He and Warren struck up a conversation and when the
custodian came back five minutes later, Granddad gave
him the signal to give them more time.

Actually, the custodian worked overtime that day, and
Granddad made sure he was compensated (out of his own
pocket), so that the visit could go a little longer – actually,
a lot longer, about five hours.

The conversation between those two men, one 20 years
old and the other 49 years old, began a lasting friendship.
On the basis of that five-hour conversation, Warren Buffett
bought his first 350 shares of GEICO stock. The meeting
between Warren and Davy was, I think, a legendary
moment in the business world.

Granddad described Warren Buffett to me with great
detail. He said he knew within the first fifteen minutes
he was speaking with a most extraordinary human being.
Along life's path, I have met many extraordinary men and
women through my Granddad, but he spoke of Warren in
a way that touched me deeply. Warren has always given
my Granddad the honor I know he deserves. Granddad
changed this young man's life, just by taking some time to
talk with him.

My granddad was right; Warren Buffett is exceptional and
he has certainly made his mark in business and in history.
When he and I met at GEICO after many years

on February 8, 2007, we spoke of our mutual love for my Granddad.

Granddad had asked me to promise to make contact with Warren again before I turned 50 and begin writing this book, a book that might motivate others through these true lessons in life and business. I kept my promise.

Davy's GEICO identification badge which he gave to his granddaughter along with his first Canadian dollar and his business cards before his death.

"What a difference the education you gave me has meant in my life."

— *Warren E. Buffett*

"Genius lights it's own fire, but it is constantly collecting materials to keep alive the flame."

— *Wilmott*

Professor Benjamin Graham, a good friend of Granddad's, a Wall Street legend and former Chairman of the Board of GEICO. *(Photo courtesy GEICO.)*

Finding Out Everything

G randdad met Warren Buffett in 1951. In those days downtown Washington was closed up tight as a drum on a Saturday. Government was closed, banks were closed, the financial district was closed, but Granddad was working that morning. He was the only person in the investment building who was working, besides the janitor. He used to like to work on Saturdays, because he found that he could do more work on Saturday than he could in any other two days of the week. His position at the time was the financial vice president.

Warren Buffett was then a student at Columbia University, taking classes from Professor Ben Graham. Granddad thought a lot of Ben. Because Warren was a student of Ben's, Granddad thought he'd give him five minutes, thank him for coming, and find a polite way of sending him on his way.

When Warren said he had come to Washington to find out everything he could about GEICO, Granddad was intrigued. Warren said that "if GEICO was good enough for Ben Graham," then there must be something in GEICO that would interest Warren very, very much.

Warren told Granddad that he was taking classes from Ben Graham. While reading Who's Who in Finance and Industry, Warren looked up Ben and found a long story with a long list of the business positions that Ben held. One of those positions had been the Chairman of the Board of GEICO. Warren thinks, even to this day, that Ben Graham is one of the greatest men who ever lived.

My Granddad thought that he would give this young man five minutes just because he was a student of Ben's, but Granddad changed his mind very quickly. After just a few questions, Granddad realized that he was talking to a highly unusual young man. The questions Warren was asking him were the questions that would have been asked by an experienced insurance stock analyst. His follow-up questions were very professional. "You wouldn't expect that type of questions from him because he was so young, and he looked younger," said Granddad. Warren described himself as a student, but he was talking like a man who had been around a long time, and he knew a great deal. Granddad's opinion of Warren changed quickly and he began asking him questions!

Granddad found out that Warren had been a successful businessman at age 16, that he had filed his own income tax return at age 13, and has filed his own income tax return every year since then. He learned that Warren had already had a number of small businesses. One of them was the operation of several newspaper routes in Omaha and in Washington. Warren's father was a broker in Omaha, but he had just been elected to Congress. So Warren really had two homes: Omaha and Washington. Warren caddied at Chevy Chase, not to earn the caddy's fees, but to be able to buy lost golf balls from the other caddies. He'd give them a quarter, polish them up, sell them for fifty cents. He had ten pinball machines, which he had placed in small restaurants and barber shops. He was buying and selling stocks, for his own account and for his sister.

Warren asked questions about all areas of business, including how premiums were written, the history of premiums, the claims paid, the production of business, even accounting points. Warren thought he was running out of time with my Granddad, but actually he wasn't. My grandfather wanted to listen to Warren. Warren would say, "Now, I'll just be a few minutes more," but then Warren would want to ask two more questions. "How do you handle the production of new business? How does GEICO underwrite?" These were two key questions, according to my Granddad, about the operation at GEICO. My grandfather then said to Warren, "If you know the answer to those two things, you know GEICO." And what started out to be a five minute chat turned into hours of talk.

After they talked about GEICO, Warren and Granddad talked about the insurance business in general and that lasted about an hour more. Then they got into what Warren called "the most important decision that I will ever have to make" and that was what was he going to do after he graduated in just four months. What was he going to do then? It turned out that what Warren really wanted to do was to go back home and work in his father's brokerage office in Omaha.

Warren told my grandfather that he didn't want to sell mutual funds for the rest of his life. Then my grandfather told Warren to go back to the family brokerage firm, and then get the "Wall Street experience," as my grandfather had done at the age of 22. My grandfather told Warren, "You have to have the Wall Street experience now - not later in life - because then, frankly, it will be too late." And that's what Warren eventually did.

Warren did, at one time, make a deal with Ben Graham; Warren told Ben that he would work for free for one year. Ben told Warren that, typically, his policy was to pay people what they were worth. He told Warren that he would be worth a lot more than nothing. He didn't accept Warren's proposition, but instead he told Warren, "I'll pay you $12,000 a year to come to work for me. At the end of that time, or at anytime, if you want to leave and go someplace else, you're free to do it." This was the completion of Warren's education in the investment business.

Warren and my grandfather ended their first conversation by talking about what Warren was going to do next. That first meeting took about five hours. Warren asked if he could visit with my grandfather again. Warren said, "I'll be sure to make an appointment next time."

Warren came to see my grandfather many times after that. They kept in touch with each other for more than 47 years, right up to the death of my Granddad. Warren and my grandfather were true friends. They talked often and saw each other occasionally. It's been a wonderful friendship for me to see through the years and I know that it has been a very valued friendship for both of them.

My Granddad told me: "Warren will go down in history with the names of Henry Ford and Andrew Carnegie, as a man who built a great fortune, starting from nothing. With that fortune, he will help a great mass of people."

Author's note: On June 26, 2006, Warren donated $37 billion dollars to five foundations, with the bulk going to the Melinda and Bill Gates Foundation. The donation represented about 80% of his personal fortune, a sum that will certainly help "a great mass of people." Granddad was right again!

"Location. Location. Location."

"This is the final test of a gentleman: His respect for others who can be of no possible service to him."
– *Richard Le Gralliene*

Coca-Cola Six Pack

G randdad told me a story of one of Warren's very rare, not too successful operations. It was the "incident of the six pack of Coca-Cola." Warren bought Coca-Cola at slightly above wholesale price, and sold it retail at a stand which he and a friend of his opened. Before they set up the stand – in a move that was typical of Warren – they researched the location, counting the cars that would pass during a certain number of hours, from 8 o'clock in the morning until 7 to 8 at night, on the street where Warren lived. And then, the next day Warren did the same thing with the street that his friend lived on.

There was more traffic on his friend's street, so that was where they established the Coca-Cola stand. Warren thought if the stand worked, he would open more of them. It didn't turn out to be just what Warren expected. They never sold enough, no matter the number of cars that passed by. Warren's second deal with Coca-Cola, was however, a little bit more successful. Today, Berkshire Hathaway, Warren's company, owns many shares of Coca-Cola. Their profit from those shares has made a great deal of money. So, the second time around for Warren with Coca-Cola was so much better than the first venture.

Warren was, and maybe still is, the biggest stock holder of Coca-Cola. And, if he talked to you for fifteen minutes today, you'd go out and buy Coca-Cola stock. Warren says he has discovered the secret: the profit in Coca-Cola is in the juice – the syrup! Forget about selling bottles of the stuff.

"A man is a worker. If he is not that, he is nothing."
                                        – *Joseph Conrad*

"There may be luck in getting a good job, but there's
no luck in keeping it."
                                        – *J. Ogden Armour*

Lorimer Davidson, president of GEICO welcomes
Preston Estep, president of the National Associa-
tion of Independent Insurers, to a convention in
Washington D.C. in 1959.

Being A Pro

There are no short cuts to being a pro. Being fully trained is not the same as being fully professional in one's job according to my Granddad. The true professional, whether a manager or a rate clerk, applies his/her knowledge and experience to the job unconsciously and almost effortlessly. The skills are so developed that the worker no longer thinks about each individual step. Instead, there is time and ability to keep up with developments in their field, with an open mind to new ideas and new methodology.

Every individual can become a pro in their job, whatever the job. But the process takes time and effort. The young doctor spends several years as an intern; the professional ball player once played on the sandlots. The golfer hits thousands of balls from the driving range.

A claims man may know the methodology involved in the settling of a claim, but even the best is still an "amateur" until she/he understands human nature so well that he can intuitively spot the truth-teller and the "exaggerator"; until she/he looks at a damaged automobile and immediately knows what the approximate repair costs will be.

One day her/his skills and the exercising of those skills and talents jell and he/she has become the best in his field – a professional.

The dictionary gives several definitions for professional, including "participating for gain or livelihood in an activity or field of endeavor often engaged in by amateurs," and "conforming to the technical or ethical standards of a profession," and "engaged in one of the learned professions."

It is possible to be a professional without being a doctor, lawyer, or professor. There are pro golfers and pro supervisors. A supervisor, may, however, be a supervisor for many years and still not be a pro. The process of becoming a professional involves, not only experience gained from time on the job, but the willingness and desire to apply both experience and available resources to that job.

A "new" quarterback may be able to throw the ball 65 yards, but still be an amateur. The professional ball player needs not only to throw the ball, but also must be able to throw to a moving target and still be able to read the defense and run while doing this. The amateur has not developed this unconscious skill. The pro football player can read the defense, avoid the defense, and throw an accurate pass. The new quarter back may be sacked before he can get rid of the ball.

If the beginner tries to use the pro's techniques, he will fail. The road to professionalism is long, usually difficult, and is reached only through practice and hard work.

The moment when a person actually passes from "amateur" to "professional" goes unheeded. There is no celebration; there will be no 100 percent mark recorded. Yet one day, said my Granddad, you may suddenly realize that you are capable of effortlessly using professional techniques, or someone will make a decision, based on certain techniques that they learned over a period of time, without being aware that they are even employing a system.

In this way, each becomes aware of their own achievement: they have "arrived". They are a real pro at last. The hard work has paid off.

It is these people who will be rewarded with the opportunity to enlarge their areas of responsibility and professionalism. The long, hard road leading to pro status has additional rewards at the end—the self-satisfaction of a goal accomplished, the deserved respect from one's co-workers, family and friends, and the acknowledgement of one's ability by peers.

y way of
ir poem (Jona-
n. [Middle Eng-
d borrowing
dimion < pro-
ong; (literally)

ductory; prefa-

dtein formed in
ve forerunner
nto an active
gen: The key
v in the blood
ne, profibrinoly-

. Zoology. the
ous cycle. [<

ssional in
dtte]
adj., n. — adj.
ial, cultural, or
ropean coun-
cooperation
t.

gious order.
pro|fes|sion|al (pre fesh'e nel, -fesh'nel), adj., n. — adj. 1 of or having to do with a profession; appropriate to a profession: Dr. Smith has a professional seriousness very unlike his ordinary joking manner. 2 engaged in a profession: A lawyer or a doctor is a professional person. 3 following an occupation as one's profession or career: a professional soldier, a professional writer. 4 making a business or trade of something that others do for pleasure: a professional musician, a professional ballplayer. 5 undertaken or engaged in by professionals rather than amateurs: a professional ball game. 6 making a profession of something not properly regarded as a profession: a professional busybody. — n. 1 a person who makes a business or trade of something that others do for pleasure, such as singing or dancing: Only one member of the band is a professional; the others are amateurs. The musician is a professional who tours the country. 2 a person engaged in a profession; professional man or woman: The medical conference was attended by both laymen and professionals.
pro|fes|sion|al|ism (pre fesh'e ne liz'em, -fesh'-

35

"Just when you are so sure you are right,
without question, that is the time to Be Quiet
and Listen. You may learn something."
– *Davy Davidson*

Warren E. Buffett

Dear Davy –
You remain the great class
act of American business. I'll
never forget the start you
gave me. Happy Holidays!
Warren

Competition – Change is Necessary

We establish challenging objectives for our continued growth. We consider our projections of new business for all our services as realistic. However, it is increasingly evident that it will require an extraordinary effort for fulfillment. The reason is all too obvious – increasingly intensifying competition.

My Granddad said that the general environment in which we sell our services has changed considerably in the last few years. Not too long ago, a company may have stood almost alone in their field. Now they find themselves surrounded by many competent and aggressive competitors. New and effective competitive devices are appearing in the marketplace, and these special features are taking the base of clientele and putting more competitive pressures on a company.

Granddad believed that to be aware of these developments is not enough. We must meet this new challenge with our long-proved ability to succeed with our maximum effort.

We can no longer expect to obtain and retain our business on the basis of a favorable rate advantage alone. Service and quality are the uncompromising demands of our customers – and they will go wherever this demand can be met.

"Spend less than you make."

– Anonymous

❧

"Perfect practice makes perfect performance."

– Rick Jones

Warren E. Buffett

Dear Davy,
Whenever I write you, I think of the great influence you have had on my life. Without the guidance you gave me early on, my career would have been much different.
Happy Holidays,
Dam

Cost Control

Certainly most everyone, said Granddad, is – or ought to be-aware of the fact that our right to business is based on our ability to keep our expense ratio low.

There will always be cost increases in taxes and in general operating expenses; that's a given. In order to offset these increased costs we must at all times remain cost conscious.

You must be alert to ways and means of controlling costs through elimination of waste and duplication. Technology can help with that if it is used wisely. The more you are able to increase operating efficiency, the more you will be able to keep your expenses in line and thus assure the retention of your competitive position.

Business can only receive so many rate increases. Eventually rate increases will no longer offset spending costs. Be aware of the profit squeeze, said my Granddad, and at all times be cost conscious.

"Live well below your means."

– Davy Davidson

"You're a Genius . . .   you're wonderful."

– Davy Davidson

"Count your blessings."

– Davy Davidson

A twenty dollar gold piece.

Great Expectations

With all the problems we have before us, in the world and market, the key to success is to have faith and trust in people who you hire, so employers hire individuals with a strong work ethic, leadership skills, and knowledge in their position – a pro. Teamwork should be demonstrated at all levels. My Granddad believed that the need for working together is more pronounced now than ever before. What has been done well in the past, has to be done superlatively now!

Teamwork & $20 Gold

There is a story that my Granddad told me about teamwork and helping someone in need. When he was young boy, during the early part of his life, a $20 gold piece was a lot of money. It took many, many hours of hard labor to earn that much money and the buying power was tremendous.

Once there were two young, teenage boys, Sam and Paul. They were your typical young boys, always having fun. One day Paul and Sam were walking down a country road near a stream, and they found an old worn out jacket, with holes. They wondered who this could belong to. Paul heard something near the stream. The two boys could see, through some bushes, an older man trying to get a drink from the running water. He was crouched down with his back to the boys, but he had removed his jacket so it wouldn't get wet. He was dressed in clothes that matched his jacket. Sam and Paul didn't recognize him because of his position facing the water. Sam came up with an idea to play a joke on this older gentlemen.

Sam said, "Let us take the jacket, hide it, and hide behind these bushes and watch what the older man does."

Paul thought about the suggestion, then replied, "I have a better idea. I have this $20 gold piece in my pocket. Let us put it in the pocket of the worn out jacket. Then, let's hide and watch this man's reaction."

Sam asked Paul, "Are you nuts? Don't you remember how long it took for you to save that much and all the work you had to do?" Paul answered, "Yes, I do, but I still want to do it."

Sam agreed reluctantly. So, Paul found the pocket of the jacket that didn't have holes in it and put in the $20 gold piece. Then the boys took their positions behind the bush and watched. As the man came through the path, the boys stared with amazement. It was Mr. McFadden, the poorest man in town. His wife was sick and he had four young children. He was on the road trying to sell anything of value to help the family finances.

As Mr. McFadden slipped his jacket on he felt something in his pocket. He reached in and pulled out the $20 gold piece. Mr. McFadden fell down to his knees and started to cry. He looked around to see if anyone was near, but he saw no one. He raised his head to the heavens and said, "Thank you, God. Now I can buy medicine for my wife and be home with my family who need me. Thank you!"

Paul and Sam had opposite ideas, but, by working together, they helped not only themselves, but also someone else. You can never tell how far reaching an effect you may have, especially when you work together as a team.

Granddad said that as we go into the future we can be assured of success if we are first aware of the nature of some of the problems confronting us and then adopt a positive and aggressive attitude toward devising their solutions. Then, you can be the greatest in the history of your company. It is up to each of us!

"God Bless America."

– Davy Davidson

"Be Proud to be an American. Learn the Pledge of Allegiance, memorize it. Honor our Flag. We are the land of the free."

– Davy Davidson

Warren E. Buffett

Hi Davy –
As the years go by, my appreciation constantly grows for the terrific people I have been helped by during my life. You are up there at the top of the list & – once again – thanks for all you've done for me. Happy Holidays + good golfing in 1991.

Warren

Freedom, Right, and Choice

The process of swearing in a President of the United States is something more than the normal and expected aftermath of a President or individual being elected or defeated. This symbolizes the right of a free people to choose, by means of a secret ballot, the man or woman they wish to have as their leader.

The choice was made and the leader inaugurated with complete understanding by all concerned that the President's policies and record will be examined four years hence to determine anew whether he, and the political party he represents, accomplished his goals.

My granddad felt that the machinery set up to be used in the choice of a President epitomizes the wisdom and fairness of the American governmental system. It signifies, he believed, the confidence and trust we in this country have in the stability of our governmental institutions, and the compliance of our political leaders to the demands of our system.

These facts are well worth remembering at this point in history, said granddad, when so many influences are at work elsewhere in the world breeding chaos and anarchy aimed at the eventual subordination, or even destruction, of individual freedom and right of choice.

As we look at the President and set ourselves foursquare behind him in the task he has of guiding the American people in these troubled days, we know we can still be constructively critical of his policies.

Granddad felt the president would take no sanctions against those who do not fully agree with him and his approach to our problems. He would, in the best spirit and tradition of all American Presidents, gracefully abide by the decision of the people, whether it is the favorable or unfavorable to his party, come next election. The political party which he leads would, in those circumstances, prove equally loyal as the "loyal opposition."

Granddad said that all of us should thank God for an America where we have the privilege of choice. He felt we should continue to honor, revere, and protect the institutions that not only reflect the sincere will of the American people, but that have been tempered through the passage of time to a point where their soundness is beyond dispute.

Davy was very proud of his American citizenship but never wanted to forget his roots. He always carried a Canadian dollar in his wallet to remind him of where he came from.

"Joy is not in things; it is in us."

– Wagner

"No question is settled until it is settled right."

– E. W. Wilcox

"If you have knowledge, let others light their candles with it."

– Anonymous

Warren E. Buffett

11-29

Dear Davy,

I just heard the sad news about Betty. Though I never really knew her, she made you happy for many decades + that gave me warm feelings for her. She was both a witness to, + a participant in, your extraordinary accomplishments + that must have provided

Giving Back

Granddad felt that every one has to do something within the community. And, it was for that reason that he accepted two invitations to join and help a great church and a great hospital.

He was a trustee of Federal City Council, which had quietly done a lot for the city of Washington D.C. and that area. Granddad was also a director of the Riggs Bank for ten years. Granddad said, "I spent many hours a month doing community service. I tried hard to give back to a community that had been so good to me."

Davy enjoying himself with other Riggs Bank directors, (1976).

"I believe in hard work, long hours of work. Man does not break down from overtime, but from worry and dissipation."

– Charles Evans Hughes

"After all, it's a great country but you can't live in it for nothing."

– Will Rogers

Warren Buffett writing about investing in GEICO stock.
(Photo courtesy GEICO.)

K.I.S.S.

G EICO was the beneficiary of amazing results from very little efforts in marketing. Their approach from the beginning was a simple card sent to people in the mail. This little card produced millions of dollars from new and renewing policy holders.

Granddad worked in the production area. His job was to produce business. Up to that time, it had been very successful on that card. It was an amazing thing – he still didn't believe it – that GEICO could send out just one little card and get the money rolling in, in millions, as they did.

Granddad had been a salesman all his life, and it is a revelation to him when he saw this little pass-along card producing all this business. As a salesman, he always had to work hard to sell. It always astonished him how GEICO gets so much business with so little effort.

He said, "It is a miracle that a relatively small company like GEICO has become so successful with so little direct sales effort." He said he learned from that little card that one of the best marketing tools is to "Keep It Simple, Stupid".

"Progress involves some risks: you can not steal second and stay on first."

– Kentucky School Journal

"Learn from your mistakes and then don't repeat them."

– Davy Davidson

Lorimer A. "Davy" Davidson, President of GEICO. *(Photo courtesy GEICO.)*

Survival by Adaptation and Thinking Outside the Box

There is no time like the present, but if some thought isn't given to the future than there won't be much of a present for long. Strategizing and positioning are key components to any successful company, but are companies willing to take a hard look at the facts and make the necessary changes to survive? That was an important question according to my grandfather.

GEICO faced one such issue in my grandfather's tenure: Should they stick with Government-only policy holders, or should they open it to the general public?

My Granddad said that following a big month in premium writings, George Peery made what he thought was a joke. George said, "If we continue to grow like this, we're going to grow out of customers pretty soon." He thought that was humorous, said Granddad, but he was making a very serious statement.

"That started us thinking about the fact that there was a limit on the number of government employees in the offices and armed forces with whom we could do business," said Granddad. They realized there were other good categories, like bank presidents, clergy, and dentists. So, after they discussed it in three or four weekly meetings, they decided to form a committee to study the question of whether or not they should expand their eligibilities.

That committee worked for nearly a year, and they did a superb job. They gathered information from every source that was available. They were able to finalize their recommendation to the board, which was well documented and proved that they could expand in a number of categories listed in a report.

It was a recommendation that received a mixed reaction. There were some directors who needed to be sold much harder than others. The fear was that, instead of being a preferred-risk company, GEICO would be just another insurance company.

"We started a company, got it going, and it was working just great. Everybody was getting rich by the company operating as it was. Why change it? But we always came back to the same point that had been raised: if we keep on doing this, we won't have as many prospects as we have today. There will be a point some years down the line, maybe a long ways out, but there will be a point where we just can't grow anymore. We'd just have to stop," said Granddad.

"The committee was right, the operations policy committee was right, and the board was right. It was a move, which was probably the most important move that GEICO ever made," he said.

Knowing when you are right, though, isn't enough. You have to know where you're going and how to get there.

Sometimes that may involve changing course, making sacrifices, and questioning everything, even the unimaginable. Change is never easy, but sometimes very necessary.

"There isn't a heck of a lot you can do to stop a machine that's going full blast in the wrong direction, but move out of its way," Granddad said.

GEICO headquarters today in Chevy Chase.

"Unselfish and noble actions are the most radiant pages in the biography of the soul."

– David Thomas

Management: Which Way?

The eternal struggle for most managers: Does the trust and confidence exist to allow employees to go and do their work without much interference, or, does a manager need to oversee almost every aspect of the business? Does this action cause undo stress?

In an interview it was once asked of Granddad if the management styles of Cleaves Rhea, founder of GEICO, and Warren Buffet were similar.

"Oh no, no, no," he responded. "Cleaves was a man who would not delegate. It was his one fault; he had great difficulty delegating. He came to Washington one day a month for one reason: to check on Leo. He couldn't just stay in Ft. Worth and say, 'Leo's doing a great job; we sure wish him well.' He had to be there and see it for himself."

This was the same with Cleaves' two banks in Ft. Worth according to Granddad, and the same with his finance company. Cleaves had a brother, A.D. Rhea, who had died several years earlier. They had worked together very, very closely. After his brother's death, Cleaves believed he had to do all the work that two of them had done before.

"Mr. Buffet, on the other hand," said Granddad, "Is exactly the opposite, priding himself on finding wonderful businesses, wonderful managers, and then leaving them alone."

How much more would our employees accomplish if we would just get out their way? What new directions would they find if we weren't hovering all of the time? How much more could we accomplish as managers if we focused on our objectives and not those that have been assigned?

Granddad always said, "You can either be part of the problem or part of the solution." That became for everyone in the family our mantra.

"My son, Tom, my only child is a Rocket Scientist."
— *Davy Davidson*

Tom Davidson, Gwyn Davidson's father, the son of
Davy and Betty.

"Thank you all for your hard work, and for smiling and saying hello to me whenever our paths crossed in the hallway."
— *Davy Davidson*

Lorimer A. "Davy" Davidson at retirement.

Stop, Smile, and Say Hello

Granddad was a hard worker, a successful executive, and an intelligent investor. One might think that taking time out of his day for anyone besides those with whom he absolutely had to speak, would be uncommon since he was so busy, but that is what made him unique and beloved by his employees.

The following are excerpts from a book given to him upon his second retirement from GEICO:

Mr. Davidson,
   It was always so nice to see your friendly face and receive a warm welcome. Your kindness is unsurpassed. By your smile and recognition you made many GEICO employees feel good, especially we the lower rank.

Mr. Davidson,
   I never worked with you, except in the most general sense that we all work for GEICO, but it has been a pleasure to pass you in the halls, exchange greetings, and to know that, even though you don't know me personally, you care about all GEICO people.

Mr. Davidson,
   Your smile and pleasing personality will be surely missed by me and all who know you.

Mr. Davidson,

Did not know you personally, but unlike many executives, you always seem to have a friendly hello to give.

Good luck to you always.

Mr. D.,

Someone once said a leader has two important characteristics: (1) He is going somewhere and (2) He is able to persuade other people to go with him.

Warm wishes to a respected leader.

Mr. D.,

Your cheerful smile, your pleasant way of always recognizing the individual as a special person are wonderful.

Bless you!

Gwyn Davidson in 1961. Davy had a WATS phone line
installed just so he could talk to his granddaughter every day.

"The trouble with our times is that the future is not what it used to be."

– Paul Valery

Warren Buffett, Melinda and Bill Gates at the announcement of Warren's donation to the Gates Foundation. *(Photo courtesy of the Bill and Melinda Gates Foundation.)*

Chip

Granddad called me one day and talked about a wonderful new technology, a technology that would revolutionize the world.

"Sweetheart," said Granddad, "Warren told me about a 'chip in Seattle.' He says it's going to be really big someday, big enough to change the world. Gwyn, do you know anything about this chip?" I did, actually, but very little. My children knew much more. I tried to explain it to Granddad but he couldn't quite fathom the idea of computers, computer software, and how it would change business forever.

But, though the computer chip was a mystery to him, the man behind the chip was someone he could understand. Granddad's stated his impression of Bill Gates quite simply: "He's the greatest inventor since Thomas Edison." Warren Buffet would tell Granddad he really didn't understand all this Microsoft stuff, either, and Granddad would say, "Yes, you do, Warren, because you are the most brilliant man on this planet."

When my daughter was eight years old she would try and e-mail her great granddad, and, teasingly, he would say, "She makes me look stupid." Then he would add, "I truly have no idea how they do these 'things' on the computer. But, I'm honored to be friends with those who do know and I guess he (Bill Gates) has *some* house in Seattle."

"All wise thoughts have been thoughts already thousands of times, but to make them truly ours, we must think them over again honestly until they take place in our own personal experience."
– *Goethe*

Gwyn and her grandfather Davy, on her birthday October 15, 1965.

The Passing of a Great Man

Warren, Tony and Bill wanted my Granddad to go to the annual Berkshire Hathaway meeting in 1998. Granddad was ill. He had cancer, and was, at that time, 96 years young and still sharp as a tack. He said at that point in his life he "just wanted to be remembered for doing something good for someone."

How many people in their lives mentor a man like Warren Buffett?

Because he couldn't go that year to the meeting, we talked about the three men who had asked him to come and Granddad's thoughts turned to Omaha, Nebraska, and he asked me to please go to the annual meeting once I got the book written. I promised I would. So, my Dad, Tom Davidson, of Ogden, Utah, and I will be there at the meeting in May of 2008.

After that promise came these words, all of which have proven to be true: "Bill and Warren are great friends. They travel to Africa together, even to China. They do a lot of good for others. Warren has a relationship with Bill similar to my relationship with Warren. We are personal friends."

"I know the future of the world is in good hands with brilliant young people, brilliant middle-aged people, and, when this is written, Warren will be in the senior citizen category, and yet, with all this brilliance, talent, and hard work, it just comes down to a few simple truths. Do what you love, do it well, and give back. And of course, be disciplined about it."

Warren Buffett talked and gave a special tribute to my Granddad at that Berkshire Hathaway Meeting in 2000. He said, "It's with sadness that I report to you that Lorimer Davidson, GEICO's former Chairman, died last November, a few days after his 97th birthday. For GEICO, Davy was a business giant who moved the company up to the big leagues. For me, he was a friend, teacher and hero. I have told you of his lifelong kindnesses to me in past reports. Clearly, my life would have developed far differently had he not been a part of it."

Warren went on to say, "Tony, Lou Simpson and I visited Davy in August and marveled at his mental alertness – particularly in all matters regarding GEICO. He was the company's number one supporter right up to the end, and we will forever miss him."

"One hundred years from now it will not matter what kind of car I drove, what kind of house I lived in, how much money I had in my bank account, nor what my clothes looked like. But the world maybe a little better because I was important in the life of a child."
                                                    – *Forest E. Witcraft*

Illustration of Gwyn Davidson Larsen and her grandfather Davy
Davidson in 1963.

Mr. Lorimer Arthur "Davy" Davidson

Favorite Quotes of Granddad

My Granddad loved and collected quotes. He thought that we should all know and be inspired by some of the greatest thinkers who put things just the right way. Certainly, he found inspiration for his work and life in them.

"A foundation of good sense, and a cultivation of learning, are required to give seasoning to retirement, and make us taste its blessings."

– Dryden

"Rest (retirement) is the sweet sauce of labor."

– Plutarch

"A reputation for good judgment, fair dealing, truth, and rectitude, is itself a fortune."

– H. W. Beecher

"Pleasure is the flower that fades; remembrance is the lasting perfume."

– Boufflers

"It is not he who searches for praise that finds it. True praise is the lot of the humble."

– Rivarol

"Give me a positive character, with a positive faith, positive opinions and positive actions."

– C. Simmons

"Our attitude tells to the world what we think of ourselves – and what we have decided to become."

– Earl Nightingale

"The ablest men in all walks of modern life are men of faith. Most of them have much more faith than they themselves realize."

– Bruce Barton

"Enjoy the acquaintance of young people and you'll never fear growing older."

– Ben Johnson

"Three days of uninterrupted company in a vehicle will make you better acquainted with another, than one hour's conversation with him every day for three years."

– Lavater

"Four things come not back: The spoken word; The sped arrow; Time past; The neglected opportunity."

– The Second Caliph

"Few men are admired by their servants. Those who are, are loved."

– Montaigne

"A person is always startled when he hears himself called 'old enough to retire' for the first time."

— *Oliver Wendell Holmes*

"Some men never grow old. Always active in thought, always ready to adopt new ideas, they are never chargeable with fogyism. Satisfied, yet ever dissatisfied; settled, yet ever unsettled; they always enjoy the best of what is and are the first to find the best of what will be."

— *Shakespeare*

"It is wonderful what strength of purpose and boldness and energy of will are aroused by the assurance that we are doing our duty."

— *Scott*

"A laugh is worth one hundred groans in the markets."

— *Charles Lamb*

"Ignorance with love is better than wisdom without it."

— *Anonymous*

"Happiness is a perfume you cannot pour on others without getting a few drops on yourself."

— *Anonymous*

"Character is the result of two things: mental attitude and the way we spend our time."

— *Elbert Hubbard*

"What sunshine is to flowers, smiles are to humanity; they are but trifles to be sure; but, scattered along Life's pathway, the good they do is inconceivable."

– Addison

"Common sense is the knack of seeing things as they are, and doing things as they aught to be done."

– C. E. Stowe

"It is right to be contented with what we have, never with what we are."

– MacKintosh

"Speak well of everyone if you speak of them at all – none of us are so very good."

– Elbert Hubbard

"Occupation is one great source of happiness. No man properly employed was ever miserable."

– L. E. Landon

"Esteem cannot be where there's no confidence; and there can be no confidence where there is no respect."

– Giles

"Tell me your convictions; I have doubts enough of my own, at times."

– Goethe

"Friendship is always a sweet responsibility, never an opportunity."

– *Kahlil Gibran*

"Life does not count by years. Some suffer a lifetime in a day, and so grow old between the rising and the setting of the sun."

– *Augusta Evans*

"To everything there is a season, and a time for every purpose under heaven; a time to be born, and a time to die; a time to plant, and a time to pluck that which is planted."

– *Ecclesiastes 111: 1-8*

"Great people are ordinary people with an "extra-ordinary" amount of determination."

– *Robert Schuller*

"Opportunity, sooner or later, comes to all who work and wish."

– *Lord Stanley*

"A room hung with paintings is a room full of thoughts."

– *Sir Joshua Reynolds*

"As every thread of gold is valuable, so is every moment of time."

– *J. Mason*

"Only that traveling is good which reveals to me the value of home."

> – *Thoreau*

"Bloom where you are planted!"

> – *Unknown*

"Like the bee, we should make our industry our amusement."

> – *Goldsmith*

"Leisure is a beautiful garment, but it will not do for constant wear."

> – *Anonymous*

"Life is like music; it must be composed by ear, feeling, and instinct, not by rule."

> – *Samuel Butler*

"The light of friendship is like the light of phosphorus, seen plainest when all around is dark."

> – *Crowell*

"Happiness is as a butterfly, which, when pursued, is always beyond our grasp, but which, if you will sit down quietly, may alight upon you."

> – *Hawthorne*

"And though in wisdom I shall grow – And many worthwhile things shall know – No matter what my learning be – Lord, make a trusting child of me."

– A. McDaniel

"Genius is the gold in the mine; talent is the miner who works and brings it out."

– Lady Blessington

"The diminutive chains of habit are generally too small to be felt, till they are too strong to be broken."

– Anonymous

"Regret for time wasted can become a power for good in the time that remains. And the time that remains is time enough, if we will only stop the waste and idle, useless regretting."

– A. Brisbane

"An acre of performance is worth the whole world of promise."

– William Howell

"One of the first things a physician says to his patients is, 'Let me see your tongue.' A spiritual advisor might often do the same."

– N. Adams

"A man should never be ashamed to own he has been in the wrong, which is to say in other words that he is wiser today than yesterday."

– Pope

"It is those acts we call trivialities that the seeds of joy are forever planted."

– George Elliott

"That best portion of a good man's life, his little nameless unremembered acts of kindness and of love."

– William Wordsworth

"Progress is the activity of today and the assurance of tomorrow."

– Emerson

"All other knowledge is hurtful to him who has not honesty and good nature."

– Montaigne

"Six essentials to abundant living: giving, forgiving, thanking, loving, praying, serving."

– Wm. Arthur Ward

"It's as easy to learn to be happy as it is to be grouchy, and there's a lot more fun in it."

–B.C. Forbes

"I owe all my success in life to having been always a quarter of an hour beforehand."

– Lord Nelson

"Today is the wise man's day; tomorrow is the fool's day – if he says 'I will do it tomorrow,' today."

– Banks

"The human race is in the best condition when it has the greatest degree of liberty."

– Dante

"Work first and then rest."

– John Ruskin

"When I want to speak let me think first, 'Is it true? Is it kind? Is it necessary?.' If not, let it be left unsaid."

– Babcock

"Reading is to the mind what exercise is to the body."

– Addison

"A man is a worker. If he is not that he is nothing."

– Joseph Conrad

"Folks who never do any more than they get paid for, never get paid for any more than they do."

–Elbert Hubbard

"He who runs from God in the morning will scarcely find him the rest of the day."

– Bunyan

"Poverty is no disgrace to man but it is confoundedly inconvenient."

– Sydney Smith

"Joy is not in things; it is in us."

– Wagner

"There are two worlds: the world that we can measure with line and rule, and the world that we feel with our hearts and imagination."

– Leigh Hunt

"We can read poetry, and recite poetry, but to live poetry is the symphony of life."

– S. Francis Foote

"The five principal moral virtues are: humility, justice, order, prudence, and rectitude."

– Confucius

"The free conversation of a friend is what I would prefer to any entertainment."

– David Hume

"If it wasn't for the optimist the pessimist would never know how happy he wasn't."

– Anonymous

"Life is a cafeteria. There are no waiters to bring you success. Help yourself!"

– Public Speakers Library

"The greatest work has always been hand in hand with the most fervent moral purpose."

– Sidney Lanier

"Go often to the house of thy friend, for weeds choke the unused path."

– Ralph Waldo Emerson

"He who cannot forgive others breaks the bridge over which he must pass himself."

– George Herbert

"My business is not to remake myself, but to make the absolute best of what God made."

– Robert Browning

"No question is settled until it is settled right."

– E. W. Wilcox

About the Author

Spending most of her younger years in and around Washington D.C., Gwyn Davidson Larsen lived many summers with her Granddad and Grandmother, where she developed a very strong bond with them. She was called their "lucky charm" because she born on their wedding anniversary. While growing up with them, she had many unique and cherished experiences.

Gwyn knows the importance of building up and enhancing the capabilities of young people. She is active in her church, working with over 15,000 young people to date. Nationally, she serves on the board of the GEICO Top Scholars, representing the Davidson Distinguished Scholars. She also serves on the Board of Treehouse Children's Museum in Utah, an organization that serves more than 150,000 children annually.

She married John Schmidt in 2003, after the passing of her first husband, Dave Larsen to Creutzfeldt-Jakob disease. John Schmidt lost his first wife, Marlynn Burningham Schmidt, to breast cancer in 2002. Together Gwyn and John have formed "The Davy Foundation." The Foundation is in honor and memory of Lorimer "Davy" and Betty Gael Davidson, and the late spouses of Gwyn and John. The Davy Foundation is a non profit organization. Proceeds from the sale of this book will be used to help children. The running of the business and its expenses are being donated by John and Gwyn in the hopes of giving to those who truly need help, right here in the United States, even more support.

Gwyn is working on two new books now. "Because I Believe," a book about surviving death, grief, and moving forward, will be published in 2008 and "Summers With My Grandparents" is slated to be released in 2009.

Please check out our website at *www.thedavyfoundation.org* and find out even more information. You can be "part of the solution and give back," too.

Gwyn Davidson Larsen at her grandfather's grave, in February, 2007.

BERKSHIRE HATHAWAY INC.
1440 KIEWIT PLAZA
OMAHA, NEBRASKA 68131
TELEPHONE (402) 346-1400
FAX (402) 346-0476

WARREN E. BUFFETT, CHAIRMAN

Ms. Gwyn Davidson Larsen
Ogden, Utah 84414

Dear Gwyn:

What a wonderful letter to receive. Clearly you have the genes of your Grandfather.

I am enclosing my final version of what I am writing about Davy in the 1999 Annual Report. Simply put, he was the best.

Sincerely,

[signature]

Warren E. Buffett

Enclosure

WEB/km

Warren E. Buffett, Chairman, Berkshire Hathaway Inc.; Gwyn
Davidson Larsen, Author; and Tony Nicely, CEO of GEICO.

Well, he did run the company!
(Courtesy GEICO.)